AF480131

the PRESENCE *of* KNOWING

A POETIC JOURNEY OF LIFE

JOHN DAVID SMITH

Cover art by Maureen Marie Sundstrom

Scribe & Canvas Publishing
South Carolina

Paperback 979-8-3484-2177-9

Published by Scribe & Canvas Publishing™
www.scribeandcanvas.com
South Carolina

Printed in the United States of America

In Loving Memory of:

Mae Ruth Jenkins Smith (1927 - 2022)
Beloved Mother, Grandmother, Aunt, Sister, and Friend.

Andy Lavern Smith (1960 - 1998)
Beloved Brother, Son, Uncle, and Friend.

I Honor You

I give honor to God for allowing me the opportunity to share this gift with you. I honor the memory of my mother, Ruth, and my brother, Andy, whose love and inspiration remain with me every day. To my family and friends who have supported me on this journey—your encouragement has been my strength.

It is my prayer that this book touches your life in a positive way, helping you realize that you are never truly alone. May these words guide you to find light in the darkness, strength in your challenges, and hope in your journey.

May God, the Creator of every good and perfect gift, bless you according to His riches in glory. May He comfort your heart, lift your spirit, and strengthen your soul.

Love and Blessings,

John David Smith

The Poet's Prelude

In the quiet spaces between words, we find the echoes of our hearts—the silent whispers that guide us through the storms and the stillness of life. This collection, *The Presence of Knowing*, is an exploration of the journey inward, a voyage through moments of joy and sorrow, loss and healing, doubt and understanding.

Each poem in this book is a reflection—a mirror to the soul, inviting us to confront the complexities of the human experience. Here, we find the faces of love, the shadows of grief, and the resilience that arises when we dare to face our deepest truths. These words are more than ink on a page; they are fragments of time, of stories told through the rhythm of life's passage, and the quiet strength of the spirit that perseveres.

This journey is not mine alone, but ours. In the space between these pages, may you find solace for your own heart, as we discover together the presence of knowing: that we are all connected through our struggles and our triumphs, our questions and our answers. And in this shared space, we are never alone.

Let the words guide you, as they have guided me. Let them speak to the depths of your soul and bring light to the corners of your heart.

Table of Contents

Love and Loss

"Through love and loss,
the heart learns its deepest lessons."

True Love

'Twould be so simple,
'Twould be so sweet,
'Twould be a gift to end a dream:

'Twould be so loved,
'Twould be adored,
'Twould be like miracles forever grown;

'Twould be a rainbow,
'Twould be a cloud,
'Twould be the sunlight in the sky;

'Twould be the nectar,
'Twould be the home,
'Twould be thy presence ever shown;

'Twould be a blessing in disguise,
'Twould be all hope no more denied:

'Twould be the vale o'er the eyes,
That shall one day leave me blind.

Falling In Love

Desperation consumes the heart,
A foggy mist controls the mind,
Nothing shall ever be clear again,
As life's perilous journey finds me blind.

Lost Love

To look into your eyes and see,
That eternal star that sparkles bright,
Bids my heart shed a tear,
For that star that lost its light.

Roaming Affection

To place my head inside cupped hands,
And place a kiss upon each palm,
To close the hands and conceal the love;
That between our hearts bid us bond;

Desires my hands to touch your crown,
And my soul peer into lily pearl eyes,
To see the joy I now hold,
And recall the love that passed 'fore time;

Lost in life's evermore embrace,
Skin kissed of the sun's sweet lips,
With stars dancing upon your face,
And clouds fading upon your hips;

Winds wrapped 'round your waist,
Bidding me closer and closer still,
Feeling the warmth of such embrace,
Comforts my soul and humbles my will;

To hold your love would reign supreme,
To feel your warmth, a cherished thought,
To express my love would soothe my being,
My will, my last, my love for naught.

As I Walked Along the Garden Path

As I walked along the garden path-
Where lovers' hearts reigned supreme,
With my heart, I felt of nothing-
So, I thought of time, and time, of me;

I envisioned places in my mind,
That once would smell of roses sweet,
But with my heart, I felt of nothing,
So, I thought of time, and time, of me;

I stole a bloom from its home,
In hopes to return to places that be-
But with my heart, I felt of nothing
So, I thought of time, and time, of me;

The wind embraced with a gentle kiss,
But a reply did not the wind receive-
For in my heart, I felt of nothing,
So, I thought of time, and time, of me;

Time – my friend – fair weathered not he,
Time stood long, I thought did he,
But time stands short – informed me did he,
Yes, time stands short, and short he be;

I've looked not once in places dreams,
Nor smelled of roses freshly groomed-
Death – my companion – my age-old friend,
Time shall introduce us soon;

In me no delay be seen,
With thee my friend I shall go-
For I've lived alone and let hearts be-

I've dreamed of dreams,
And places unseen-
For in my heart, I felt of nothing-
So, I thought of time, and time, of me.

That Summer Breeze Was Once Mine

That summer breeze was once mine,
That breeze that smelled of roses sweet,
I knew not the day or time,
Though I dwelled beneath her feet;

That summer breeze was once mine,
'Twas so vibrant, flamboyant and sweet,
I long to retrieve that day from time,
Though time vows to never retreat;

To retrieve that day to have again,
That angel of summertime rays,
Would be to me an ongoing dream,
The end to all the lonely days;

That summer breeze was once mine,
Though it matters not, I hold no more,
That rose so sweet belongs now time,
And I shall love, nevermore.

Tomorrow's Another Night

Streets of ramped quests be known,
As foresight deemed an ugly sight,
All the virtue heard by air-
Shall see the virtue lost by night;

As moonlight shines and stars subside,
Sunlight wanes to bid us pass,
But as the night welcomes the day,
A love lost once shall yield again.

Tomorrow's Dreams

Glowing hair and glistening skin,
Wandering eyes and immaculate grace,
Bids assurance of noonday's light,
And yields acceptance to tomorrow's dreams.

Don't Let Go

When you meet that certain someone,
That melts your heart from inside,
Hold her close and keep her safe,
So loneliness shan't find you blind.

Wanton Fight

As I look into your eyes,
I see a life that's vibrant and true,
I would give my life for that love divine,
If only just to be with you;
But if I gathered up all my dreams,
And offered them unto you,
They still would not be enough,
To win a heart so pure;
So I dream a dream that's mine if true,
And fill the days with crescent nights,
I bid the moon your guardian child,
And deem my heart your will to fight;
I blow a kiss into the wind,
Watch it float across the skies,
See it land upon your face,
As my heart doth slowly die.

As I Look into Your Eyes

From day to day, I think of you,
As the sun comes up and begins to fall,
Throughout the nights I dream of you,
And place wishes upon falling stars;

I awake in the mornings with rays of hope,
That maybe you shall come back to me,
For I feel as though I am blinded,
By loves lost purity;

To hold your warmth once again,
And whisper softly into your ear,
Would be to me a dream come true-
The ultimate decree of yesteryear;

And as I recall your vibrant eyes,
I see the place I belong,
And as my pulse fades away,
I shall only die in your arms.

For What Shall I Defend My Heart?

For what shall I defend my heart?
For whom shall I retreat this day?
It matters not the swerving part,
Of me that's laid along the way;

Nevermore to love again,
Or taste a gentle kiss,
Or see the dawn of daylight's end,
Or place upon the moon a wish;

That somewhere down the road I find,
A breathing piece of heart misplaced,
By someone true and still refined,
And blessed with beauty, love and grace:

But maybe I shall love the eyes,
That bid love die, and die, doth I.

Another Dream

To lay my head upon your breasts,
To breathe the same breath you breathe,
To emulate a heart that is laid to rest,
By the love of my dreams.

Last Will

The midnight sky so deathly bright,
As to bid my heart fade away,
My final plea before I die,
In your hands my love be laid.

No More Hearts

Nevermore shall I ask again,
Nevermore shall I demand-
That any woman give her heart,
To the heart of man;

It has taken many broken hearts,
To soothe the pain of the other,
It has taken many painful nights,
To erase the thoughts of another;

No longer can I fall in love,
No longer can I hold a hand,
That one day may turn against me,
And seek a wealthier hand;

I've given all I can,
I have nothing left,
Another heart has been betrayed-
And yet again introduced to death;

One last hope, one last gasp,
A final inspiration to the soul,
My heart has lost the last drop of blood,
And my body shall remain cold;

No more feelings to be expressed,
No more grief to be shared,
No more love to be shown,
No more hearts to be spared.

I Dreamed of Dreams

Once in life I dreamed a dream,
That you and I would always be,
Regardless of the day or time,
Nothing mattered, just you and I;

You were once my loyalty,
My true and honest heart,
But then our love was ended,
And along with it, my heart;

Every now and then,
I find myself wishing,
That you were somehow here again,
And nothing more was missing;

To have you near me,
Would once again prove divine,
But now my dreams have ended,
And along with them, desire;

I wish I could hear your voice again,
And see your caring smile,
I wish I could place a tender kiss,
Upon your naked brow;

But all the dreams I dreamed of you,
And all the dreams I dreamed I could,
None could sway old time undo,
All the things I wished it would.

Humble Dreams

To place a kiss upon your lips,
To gaze into your eyes,
To run my fingers through your hair,
And place a kiss upon your brow;

To have my heart become engulfed,
By the warmth of your smile,
To have my breath taken away,
By the grace under which I bow.

If Only for A While

Long flowing hair glistening in the sun,
A vibrant smile graces your face,
Without a care and no regard,
For the hearts that bid you stay;

Stay very near and do not leave,
For too many hearts die this way,
For a beautiful smile or wink of an eye,
From that breath taking glow that begins to play;

Frolic briefly and reality comes soon,
For my heart cannot bear the pain,
The very idea of a fantasy's end,
Shall with my heart forever remain;

Do not tease or taunt my lonely form
For a fragile frame does conceal,
That true emotion that seems without,
The very concept that is real;

Be favorable and do not leave,
Grace my presence with your smile,
Forget all others that you've laid to rest,
And come home to stay with me awhile.

Do Not Take Those Lips Away

Do not take those lips away,
That are so tender to the touch,
Nor those lips that bid me stay,
For I desire to stay so much;
A tender kiss again and again,
Seals my love forever, an end.

Cycle of Love

To see a sunset wane before,
The coming of the moonlit dawn,
Would be a wish granted more,
Than any wish I've ever known;

To love again my heart doth yearns,
To feel another precious touch,
To breathe again the rose sweetened air,
That upon a time meant so much;

The beauty of a day and blessedness of a night,
Would save any heart that truly believed-
That somewhere within the shadows of light,
Rests the companion for which it bleeds;

For if I owned a start that belonged to the night,
And controlled the day, sun and all,
I would give everything to be with you,
If but for a moment, would relinquish it all;

For to look into your eyes and find,
The one I'd search for all my life,
Would bring an end to a tedious past,
And begin my journey of love again.

Nothing Less Than My Very Own

So captivating and yet withdrawn,
From the world into self-
To place a picture upon your mantle,
Or a book upon your shelf;

So seductive and yet refined
So cunning and so wise,
To be the face upon which you smile,
To remove my heart and claim it thine;

So soft and tender and yet unbound,
By any man or beast be seen,
To place a kiss upon your brow,
To be the creator of your dreams;

For all the things in the world be known,
As trinkets or gifts of admiration or love-
I beseech your heart upon this day,
To be nothing less than my very own.

Sonnet 5

Hearts may bleed without a doubt,
Of what in the world is going on-
Hearts may bleed as they turn about,
To see the coming of the dawn;

For what shall I defend my heart?
For whom shall it be freed this day?
For what shall it be ripped apart,
And laid alone along the way?

Since everything doth has a past,
And every past a present,
Why be first and not the last,
For whom the arrow's meant?

My heart's been laid upon this rock,
A lonely bird without a flock.

The gallantry of tenderness,
The yearning from idolatry,
Bids an angel a goddess,
From friendship stems humanity;

Like Casanova or Don Juan,
The flame that drove Lothario,
From sea-to-sea adoration,
The gallant lover Romeo;

Through paramour a liaison,
From sympathy and fellowship,
An arrow from Cupid's bow flown,
For enrapture and engagement:

There's inclination through desire,
And romance comes to those admired.

Fleeting Desires

Stainless steel papers with edges bare,
Expose the truth we often forbear.
They leave no protection from strong desire,
A pulse ignited by an unseen fire.

A tingle felt upon the wrist,
And in the sky, a flood of roses bloom.
Their fragrance lingers, dispelling the gloom,
A touch so brief, yet impossible to resist.

Yet, like the roses, they fade too soon,
Carried away by the fleeting moon.
Desire burns, but time steals its glow,
Leaving behind a memory to grow.

The Rose in Ruins

Mystical torches upon blood-drenched walls,
Flicker in silence, where shadows call.
Catastrophic irony develops hope,
In the ruins of despair, we learn to cope.

Idealistic regions of war-torn souls,
A sweet-smelling rose blooms, breaking the chain.
Yet even here, amidst the pain,
Weary and scarred by life's harsh tolls.

Through the echoes of battle, soft winds blow,
Urging the heart to let go and grow.
Lead not to doubt, nor fear the fight,
For hope can bloom in the darkest night.

Nature's Whispers

*"The earth speaks in gentle rhythms,
inviting us to listen."*

Let the Snowflakes Fall

Let the snowflakes fall where they may,
Do not disrupt their path,
For the journey is long that they make,
And their life shall not last;

Let the snowflakes fall where they may,
So they shall gather together to keep warm,
For when it shall come the break of day,
Their journey will be done;

Do not hinder the lovely spirits,
That bid us peace and happiness,
Their earthly life – long finished since,
They need not return to distress;

Yet they do so often visit,
To see just what they left,
And then return home again,
But neither blinded, dumb or deaf;

Let the snowflakes fall where they may,
For the time shall come when you wish this true,
For on that brilliant, delightful day,
Maybe the journey will include you too.

Flower Bed

32

Red roses bloom where weeds doth grow,
With pedals glistening in the sun,
Drenched from the rains that from the heavens doth pour-
Only to shed teardrops for hearts wrongly done.

Home

On the rim of Saturn's rings,
Through Jupiter's core I do fly,
Out to Pluto and beyond-
The deepest regions where sirens sing,
Where rainbows kiss the sky,
There is where I belong.

I've Seen Dawn and Sunset

I've seen dawn and sunset on moors and windy hills,
I've seen romance spring from barren fields,
I've seen lions dance on Mt. Vernon's Peak,
I've seen the sun cry and the moon bleed,
I've seen dawn and sunset on moors and windy hills,
I've seen romance spring from barren fields.

Moonlight

Always flowing ever so bright,
With thousands of companions by your side,
Never alone on any given night,
Idealistic of a life's transitive guide.

As Treetops Catch My Wandering Eyes

As treetops catch my wandering eyes,
And my weary body bids me rest,
I slowly contemplate the mildewed skies,
As I place my hand upon my chest;

Weary body, so broken and worn,
Cannot control fatigues cruel flight,
To set asunder the cotton skies,
Under which I bed for the night;

The woods here all seem at peace,
With themselves and the stranger here,
Though be I far from home this night,
On the darkest evening of the year;

I find myself settling down,
And erasing my mind of all unrest,
I close my eyes and begin to drown,
My wanton spirit in nature's nest;

The treetops glisten from new fallen snow,
And the animals whisper in my ear,
No pain I feel in head or chest,
I'm glad I slumped by body here;

It's so nice and warm,
And the moon's shining bright,
I believe I shall remain here for the night,
I believe I shall remain here for the night.

The Seasons Tale

Flowers bloom throughout Winter's course,
As Summer's eve dawns once more-
Springtime's pow'r yields an end,
To Autumn's undying, relentless wind;

Flowers bloom throughout Winter's course,
As vagrants shimmer throughout the night,
Shadows live in crevices dim,
Protected eternally from brilliant light;

As Summer's eve dawns once more,
Hearts are warmed by deceitful touch,
Fleshes bloom throughout Winter's course;

Springtime's pow'r yields an end,
To sweet smelling tulips growing still,
Within each bud yearns another,
And flowers bloom throughout Winter's course;

To Autumn's undying, relentless wind,
Victory is granted and highly endorsed,
By all those loves never retained-
As flowers bloom throughout Winter's course.

Where Wild Roses Bloom
at Close of Day

Where wild roses bloom at close of day,
And tulips snap at your fingertips,
There, there is where our love shall stay;

Savages pose no threat along the way,
As I place my hand upon your hip,
Where wild roses bloom at close of day;

I shall put the sun, moon and stars at bay,
As the treetops tease the skyline's tip,
There, there is where our love shall stay;

As I gently listen to the words you say,
As whales, porpoises and dolphins flip,
Where wild roses bloom at close of day;

Where many a man on a sand-locked bay,
Tossed pebbles in a pond and counted each skip,
There, there is where our love shall stay;

And all that is hungry purges in the hay,
And all dried out takes a dip,
Where wild roses bloom at close of day,
There, there is where our love shall stay.

Rolling Waters

As the waters roll upon the ocean floor,
And the moistened sands move asunder,
I submerge myself in your overflowing love,
And allowed to drown without losing another.

The Unanswered Storm

Crescent rains fall amiss,
Carried by winds, unseen by eyes.
Would all of nature fall behind,
A dance of nature's soft disguise?

The clouds that refuse to weep or find
Shadows cast by day's last flight.
Their place beneath the waning light,
For in the clouds, a secret lies.

As rain falls soft, yet never clear,
We search for answers, but none appear.
A mystery behind the storm's rise,
Yet still, the question lingers near.

Oceans of Birch Bead the Earth

Radiance gleams from star-front doors,
As oceans of birch bead the earth,
Where years of growth stain man's time,
And each new past loses worth;

With each sunrise comes amends,
For which a past seems no more,
The effervescent flight of man,
Radiance gleams from star-front doors;

As oceans of birch bead the earth,
And the moon forces the daylight home,
No man shall see the breech of time,
Nor the birth of Heaven's Rome;

But as the day turns to night,
And the clouds turn to stars,
Each man who views the birth of time,
Shall see radiance gleam from star-front doors;

Where years of growth stain man's time,
And each new past loses worth,
Radiance will gleam from star-front doors,
And oceans of birch shall bead the earth.

I bathed in the Euphrates before life began,
I made my home near the banks of the Congo,
During long winter nights,
I looked upon the Nile and built pyramids before it,
In the days when the Tyger was a mere helpless child;

I danced on the waters before separate worlds were made,
Back in the days when the Tyger was a mere helpless child,
I sang lullabies to the Mississippi whenever it became enraged,
As I took my rations from the depths of the Nile,

When the time had come when days and nights were warm,
I'd pack up my home and leave for awhile,
I'd follow the Rivers great and lay praise upon their banks,
In those days when the Tyger was a mere helpless child.

Vision Beyond Sight

In darkness deep, the music shone,
Each sound a step beyond the veil—
A world unseen, yet known by ear,
Where sight was left to light the heart.
The music grew as vision failed,
A gift that reached where eyes could not,
As if he held a brighter truth,
As if in sound he saw the stars—
A sight beyond the silent dark.

Legacy in the Air

He left no stone, no word unturned,
A brilliance felt in breath and bow—
His fame, a whisper through the world,
A music bright and timeless spun.
What lingers now is not his name,
But sounds that rise beyond his time—
A resonance that wakes the soul,
A melody, both swift and pure,
A genius known in every chord.

Silent Strength

With pen in hand, he carved the truth,
Each line a mark that filled the air—
A quiet power, steady, sure,
A testament in ink and sound.
He knew the weight of form and line,
A wisdom deep, restrained, refined;
His proof lies not in words or fame,
But in the order notes can hold—
A strength that shaped the wild to calm.

Two Souls in Song

One carved his voice with strings and wood,
The other sang through softened keys—
Together bound by art's wild spark,
Their music, fierce, yet tender, free.
His fingers flew, while others sighed,
Their passions pure, their voices strong—
The bow, the song, a kindred bond,
Two souls who met where sound takes wing,
Their song, a memory that still sings.

The Dance of Shadows

Among the giants, he took form,
A presence bright, a master's hand;
His shadows long on every stage,
A force that grew beyond the sound.
His fingers played with fervor, fire,
A brilliance few could understand—
Among the great, his legend lives,
A ghostly hand on every chord,
His music wild, his spirit bold.

The Legacy in Shadow

Among the giants, he carved his place,
A presence bright, a master's hand;
His music echoed through the years,
A force that grew beyond the sound.
With fingers fierce, he shaped the flame,
A brilliance few could understand—
Among the great, his legend lives,
A spirit bold, forever grand.
In every note, his shadows dance,
A lasting trace, a whispered trance.

The Quiet After the Storm

The echoes fade, the notes grow still,
His weary hands at last released;
For every sound he shaped with care,
There rests a silence full and deep.
No wealth or fame, his life grew dim,
Yet in his heart, the music stayed—
A beauty held beyond his years,
His broken hands, his spirit strong,
A song that lives beyond his rest.

The Spirit of Sound

From sunsets in the morning,
To sunrise during the nights,
To share with thee a gift fulfilled,
Though merely a shadow of worlds aside;

Hearing wisdom etched in canvas,
Seeing His voice penned in ink,
Reminiscing on brilliance and majesty,
Flowing from hearts too vast to think;

What are the shadows our ears observe?
What's in the hand of our strength?
What is the weight our eyes cannot hold?
What's in the dust of who we are?

Our lives are filled with vibrant colors,
Yet we dream in black and white,
Our hearts are filled with words unending,
And pictures reveal the depth of our sight.

Echoes of Self

"In the mirror of life, the soul finds its truth."

I've Known of Sparrows

I've known of sparrows:
Sparrows of age and of youth-
Whose desires course through my veins.

I've known of sparrows great and small,
Full of love and vibrant embrace,
To share their joys-
To erase the pain,
To be a sparrow on freedom's wings.
Where sorrow grows but purges not.
Where heartbreaks die as faded dreams.
To share their joys-
To erase the pain.
To be that sparrow that flies away.

I've known of sparrows:
Sparrows of age and of youth-
I've known of sparrows-
I've lived the truth.

Thy True Self

There! There in the mirror!
Do you see it!?
Do you see the beast that stares back at me?!
There! There in the mirror!
Do you see it?!
Do you see in its' eyes the pity and the greed?
Look deep my friend for I know it's there!
Look deep my friend do not be scared.
Look into its' eyes and see its' soul,
Look into its' eyes and you will know-
What the beast is that looks back at me.
Look into its' eyes and you too can see.
What the beast is that looks back at me.
There! There in the mirror!
Do you see it?
Yes you do.
For the beast that stares back at me-
Is you.

Drifting

55

Eternal greatness lights my way,
And steers me from the paths of sin,
But if the darkness consumes the day,
I may be lost and never found again.

Across the Edge

I've seen the edge and thought of life,
In life I've seen reality
Across the edge I've seen night.
I may not reach my destiny
But I shall not escape my fate,
For I've see the edge and thought of life
In life I've seen reality,
Across the edge I've seen night.

I've Never Flown to Paris

I've never flown to Paris,
Nor bathed on the coast of France,
Yet I know where the Tower's anchored,
And have dreamed of sun-steeped sands;

I've never glided upon the earth,
In days of cold, blinding view,
I've never lived by others worth,
Nor tasted of natures forbidden fruit;

I've never galloped on an iron horse,
Nor danced a dance within palace walls,
Yet fast, I know, the iron horse trods,
And love remains the dance of choice;

I've never loved in Athens, Rome,
I've never sailed the open sea,
But convinced am I of hearts of gold,
And how vast the bounty be.

What Am I?

On this day I have lost my serenity,
My security, my determination and my desire;
I have abandoned any virtue and all values,
Over my life I have accomplished nothing,
Changed nothing and forgotten all;
I have placed all whom I love
In shackles of my own;
I have become a prisoner of what I
Have fled for many years;
I have become a dance partner with failure;
I have chosen once again the wrong path,
And now all those paths are converging:
I have come to the crossroads in my life,
I fear the inevitable,
Dream the impossible;
Desire the untouchable,
And walk alone for the rest of my journey;
I thread upon the waters unseen by man,
Untamed by nature,
And untouched by the hands of God;
I am the pathway to nothingness,
I am the hollow grave never filled,
I am the star that never falls,
I am the man never loved,
I am the silence in the night,
I am the winged, featherless bird,
I am the star that lost its light,
I am the forbidden fruit of earth.

Chains of Greed

Dungeons used and shackles bound,
Whips suppress the dying sound.
Freedom calls, a distant plea,
Yet greed remains the iron key.

Oppression thrives where hearts are found,
Suppressing the need to break and flee.
And still, the world spins round and round,
Where shackles fall, but none are free.

For in the fight for what is free,
We lose ourselves in tyranny.
The silence grows, a dark decree,
While justice sleeps in misery.

Shades of Loss

Shades of green, a hope once bright,
Long lonely days and dismal nights.
Now fade in shadows, lost from sight,
As the heart succumbs to fading lights.

Shades of blue, a dream once pure,
Turn to red, a hue unsure.
With every step, the world's sharp tread
Draws closer to black, where lies the dead.

Yet, in this darkness, a flicker remains,
For even in sorrow's darkest thread,
A silent spark within the chains,
Hope's whisper lingers, though faintly fed.

The Strength of Silence

Forbearance of thought shall reign supreme,
We re-evaluate the onset trough.
The silence grows, a distant dream,
Where once the sorrow seemed so rough.

As we begin to recall our speech,
A place where minds and hearts can reach.
Of exquisite pain and softened breach,
Now lessons rise, within our reach.

In every tear, a strength is born,
From fractured hearts, the spirit's sworn.
To rise again, to find the dawn,
And face the truth that time has drawn.

Return to Rest

Cotton-filled pillows of moistened clay,
Expand and contract to allow release.
A sense of escape from all that binds,
Breathe life into dreams that fade away.

The weight of the world is softened here,
A point of return to the self we find.
As reality's grasp begins to clear,
In the quiet, the soul is free.

To drift, to rest, to simply be,
Back to the truths we've long since shed.
From fiction's hand, we're gently led,
A gentle rhythm, a moment's peace.

Purity

The integrity or truth,
So idealistic and modest-
That every aspect of pudicity,
Leaves distillation leaching;

Clarifying the defecator,
And filter of sieve,
As to refine sublimation-
A percolate being;

Strain to see the unblemished stars,
That in the eyes of man are seen,
As nothing more than untainted hearts,
And lixiviation of glanderous screen;

Uncorrupted, genuine, real and true,
A simple, perfect and spotless gem
Through nothing but depilation, love and virtue,
To declassify, wash and cleanse the sin;

It shall be known upon this day,
That the vestal, lily and recent shame,
Shall no longer go without decay,
From a guiltless and innocent name;

Unadulterated, clear, lixiviated and clean,
A decorous and delicate sinless heart,
Bids a heart awaken that dream,
By which an unalloyed realm be part;

On the outskirts a virtuous chaste,
From whence shall come a wholesome denial,
When all of nature's splendors filtrate,
To become that one incorruptible child.

Patience

One petit informant full of love
divine, bids every heart to consume
a plate, by which all of nature shall
eternally endure, the hope and wishfulness of a dying trait;
Pretend ole heart that nothing succeeds,
the very absence of thy birth – Pretend
ole heart that nothing defends, the unpretentiousness
that around your peace still burns.

Resolution

Grave depressions upon lukewarm seas,
Bids assurance from yesterday's grief,
But without regard for noondays light–
Acceptance denied upon bended knees;

Farewell my friend for I retreat,
Nevermore to request your touch–
As the New Year begins and the old is past,
May our hearts find love upon nature's rock.

Sonnet 10

There's nothing more resounding,
Than the speech of the impaired-
There's nothing more a profound thing,
Than what is to be dared;
Can one ever see the truth,
Behind what is not there?
Will one ever know the truth,
And simply never share-
The understanding never seen,
Throughout the world below,
Or what is oft' found in a dream?
For we may never know;
Exactly what the world's misplaced,
Exactly how it fell from grace.

Grace in Silence

Statuettes of grace held captive from within,
A fragile strength masked by careful skin.
Wanton and depressed, hidden from view,
The sorrow unspoken, yet deep and true.

The weight of their pain rests beneath a smile,
Hiding their heart from the world's cruel ask.
A traveler's dream lost in the mile,
Poised and prominent, their mask, their task.

Yet, in the stillness, a truth is found—
In silent grace, they rise from the ground.
For even in sorrow, strength can bloom,
A quiet power that fills the room.

Eternal Weavings

And in its weave, eternity is sown,
A testament to all we've come to be.
Each life a thread, yet never stitched alone—
Together bound, one endless tapestry.
In threads of time, we find our strength and place,
The weave of life, a dance of joy and pain,
A fabric rich with stories, full of grace—
Through each connection, we rise, we fall, we gain.
And in this endless weave, our hearts are tied,
A legacy in each thread we leave behind.

Wondering

To see a rose with pedals lost,
To smell a fragrance no longer sweet,
Would bid my heart wonder on,
To find the answer of a love's defeat.

Life's Final Musings

*"Every step brings us closer to
understanding life's end—and its new beginnings*

My Age-Old Friend

Death has become my companion,
Death – my age-old friend
That one persuader who never left me,
Hears all my cries and holds my hand.

Death has become my companion
And before me lights the way
Along the path upon which I walk
By the thought of night and smell of day.

Death has become my companion
Death – my age-old friend
That vibrant star upon the sky
Who soothed my heart from loves harsh pain.

Death has become my companion
Death – my age-old friend
That one persuader who never left me
In him no sorrows remain;

Death has become my companion,
Death – my age-old friend.

If You Could See

74

If you could see the pain in my eyes,
You could see the tears.
If you could see the shadows in my life,
You could see past the years.
If you could see the hurt I hold in my hands,
You could see the tenderness they possess.
If you could see the love that breaks my heart-
You, too, would bid death a welcomed guest.

If Ever A Time

If ever a time,
When death be wished,
This is that time;

If ever a time,
With forfeiture of kiss,
This is that time;

If ever a time,
When apathy rules the mind,
This is that time;

If ever a time,
When no care be found,
This is that time;

And if ever a time,
When a lonely heart dies,
Let the last heart to die be mine.

Nevermore

Monarch butterflies so colorful and discreet,
Carrying the weight of the world upon their wings,
Throughout history together they've flown,
Beneath the skies and across the seas;

Portraits of grace and beauty foretold,
Like gates of passion in the midst,
To observe the flight with great reprise,
And smell a rose with fragrance sweet;

To join them in their sacred quest,
To find the richness in the world,
Without a doubt to revive the heart,
To grow within through the soul;

No man would dare contest,
The validity of beauty in flight,
For when their eyes are fixed in space,
The colorful discretion is mounted high;

Monarch butterflies so colorful and discreet,
Carrying the weight of the world upon their wings,
Nevermore shall I ignore the masses,
Nevermore shall I yield defeat.

Failure

Slow moving never stopping,
Always slipping never falling,
Getting shot but never dying,
Always blessed but never living,
Always forgiven but never forgiving.

Existence

To take my life would be of ease,
But for what shall I end my dream?
To confront that final circumstance,
That all the while has been seen.

Fortune

Oyster shells found intact,
Cracked and bruised to force apart,
One after the other is killed by day,
Only to retrieve the black pearled heart.

No Reminder Needed

Dark blue skies and reddish-green seas,
Give way to midday and the moons' dying light,
The sun drips of red and the sands sink low,
Just to remind you of the end;

The rodents of the earth by groups they grow,
Nature's precious birds lose their wings and fall,
Homesteads crumble under hands of stone,
Just to remind you of the end;

To see the day you're judged and tried,
Will your heart survive the last spoken word?
To see your friends who fled and died,
Just to remind you of the end;

The knowledge of knowing such a cause be found,
Just to remind you of the end,
The presence of knowing your journey's past,
That day on earth I shall not spend.

The Hand of Woe

Optimum literacy contingent upon,
The outcome of the seven seas,
By which no man on earth be known,
Through thought or sight, by word or deed;

Something unique occurs but once,
By chance sometimes and sometimes not,
To use foresight and lots of hope,
To assure the moons' correct spot;

Effervescent lighting may lead astray,
The misty-eyed would-be night,
A gentle breeze from the ocean rolls,
And gives security to a judgmental flight;

From the corner depths a hand is raised,
To yield an answer of which is true,
A heartfelt somber hardens the soul,
And red glares emerge from seas of blue;

Nevermore to be played a fool,
As an iron clad fist is anchored low,
First the love that stole a heart,
And then the thief of the soul;

As the midnight mass begins to grow,
And all of nature begins to cry,
All glowing of eyes shall bear witness,
To the hands that carried the lies.

The Final Spin

One by one, the clip is filled,
The clock ticks forward, a steady pace.
As it's placed again inside its brace,
A life's journey with purpose, fulfilled.

A final spin upon the wheel,
Shall we ponder what's left behind,
Or simply accept the peace we find?
The end of the road, the final seal.

For every race must one day end,
Now rests in the silence we must make.
The journey, though brief, was ours to take,
A life's circle, we cannot bend.

Sands of Time

A golden chamber long and precise,
Protects fine glass against default,
As the sands of time remain enclosed,
Within the fortress so divinely sought;

Gold studded columns stand erect,
As to hold up the mighty chamber,
Mounted upon a marble plate,
That bonds time to earth and stranger;

And if the chamber at once is turned,
Then time is allowed to proceed on,
To continue in its daily quest,
To announce the coming of the dawn;

But if one day that chamber's removed,
Or the glass is forced to break,
Then there shall go the sands of time,
And no more columns shall ye make;

And if the chamber is balanced off,
Then all of time will stand still,
Never to move forward again,
Unless be of greater will;

So, remember as ye pass by,
To give the chamber another turn,
For if the sands are allowed to stop,
A mighty lesson will ye learn.

My Eyes Closed Twice
Before I Died

My eyes closed twice before I died,
Once it was to love-
The other was to life.

At the entrance I stood blind,
Marveled the beauty of Heaven-
And cherished the passing of night.

My eyes closed twice before I died,
Once it was to love-
The other was to life.

At the entrance I stood deceived,
Thought upon the past,
And sank into my dreams.

My eyes closed twice before I died,
Once it was to love-
The other it was to life.

At the entrance I gave a plea
That I should die
And only me.

That I should die for all man's sins
That I should die
And nev'r love again.

My eyes closed twice before I died,
Once it was to love-
The other was to life.

Waiting

The sky's gray mass covers the land,
As the subsequent cries of man are heard,
Throughout the barren wastelands of time-
And among the flocks of pestilent birds;

The unforeseen occurrence a mist,
Dramatic pursuance of life,
Continues to bring about,
The most natural high;

Not everyone understands,
The most important thing in our time,
Everyone's priorities are different,
Everyone suffers for their crimes;

I can hope and I can pray,
That one day I shall see,
The very existence of something so true;

I continue on day after day,
Just waiting and waiting to be,
The man in the life of someone like you.

Blessed

Ever growing always wise,
Without regard for alibis,
With no regret of circumstance,
Without concern for loves last glance;

One fair day across the land,
When Cupids' arrow pierced a man,
A heart bled freely without remorse,
As emotions raised up and joy poured forth;

For something unique for something true,
For something used for something new,
For something small for something wide,
For someone else by our side;

From afar our hearts expand,
And a diamond is placed upon the hand.

Sonnet 2

To what can I compare thee?
To what I do not know-
How much time will I spend with thee?
To whether shall I go?

Is it to be the will of God?
Shall I decide my destiny?
As the muddied pathway of light I trod,
And all my life a calamity;

Return, oh light, and guide my way,
Please take my hand and lead me on-
Please make tomorrow another day,
By which I see the setting sun;

And by my side please leave a place,
For the one in my life, with an untouched face.

Dipping into realms unknown,
In realms where all has been disturbed,
Where forth shall thy will be shown?
Allow for nature to be heard;

Eyes shine bright and heart's aglow,
As though the heavens opened up,
While we journey to and fro,
The doors to Heaven are closed shut;

Admittance gained by key alone,
But not of silver or of brass,
Shall the key by man be known?
If not, our journey be our last:

Heart's aglow but not as much,
For we have lost that precious touch.

Untitled 52

I traversed the desert not long ago,
As the sun shone bright,
And the sands burned below;
From one sanctum to the next,
For miles and miles that parchment stretched,
And when the sun bowed to moonlight's grace,
Purgatory yielded to view Heaven's face;
The sands got cold, cold and colder still,
And there we stood without a will,
And there we stood without a will.

Untitled 56

I slept in the bosom of Heaven,
Upon my grateful birth,
I struggled through life,
And followed the stars,
And never got what I was worth,
As days passed on and nights unfurled,
I danced with the devil in his domain,
But material goods have little value to me,
So I sleep in the bosom of Heaven again.

Sonnet 14

Denying what too has been seen,
Regarding everything we know,
And the truth behind the dream,
In which the moon rescinds its' glow;

One small room and one small boy,
No windows open or doors to close,
No lights be found amongst the joy,
Upon which he shall write his prose;

Still blue waters remain supreme,
As light from moon above doth shine,
Upon a star begin to dream,
In hopes that true love he shall find;

Upon a day of great reprise,
It shall be for love he dies.

The Cycle of Seasons

To spend a life without reprise,
Would bid a death to autumn's glow.
From crescent nights and summer skies,
And bring spring's love to an untimely end.

For in each season, life unfolds,
Yet without autumn, spring would fade.
A tapestry that weaves through cold,
For time's embrace cannot be swayed.

To know that every end must come,
For after winter's silent song,
Is to find peace in what's been done.
Spring will bloom again, where we belong.

Flights of the Soul

"The heart sings its truest song
when it dares to fly."

Love's Peace

As the rains traverse your silken breech,
The stars twinkle and shed their skin,
The moon shines bright and full into night,
And the winds forever cool the love drenched sands.

There Is a Twinkle in Her Eye

There is a twinkle in her eye,
By which the stars yield their glow,
A star's dust captured from the sky,
That bids that twinkle continue to grow:
There embedded in her eye,
The jewel that causes hearts to cry;

That jewel's never released for any time,
If lulled by heart, soul or mind,
It just sparkles there sublime,
Waiting and waiting for one to find:
Yet prince nor king neither can buy,
The jewel that causes hearts to cry;

Her smile like angels glowing still,
Her face a rose in kingdoms stand,
Luring the weak and laden will,
And leaving them with empty hands:
That precious jewel of the sky,
The jewel that causes hearts to cry.

My Lady, My Love

My lady, My love,
My vibrant morning star,
Does not my love implore you-

To stay with me forever,
And never stray too far?
For so many ways I adore you;

My lady, My love,
Once again enchant me,
With the voice that I adore:

Think of our song,
And once again lull me,
To that sweet celestial shore;

Sing My lady,
Sing My love,
Sing to me once more:

Find those words,
That cause moonbeams,
To dance upon the shore;

My lady,
My love,
Allow your song to kiss me:

Again,
And again,
Sweet roses never miss me:

I shall cry for you,
If you desire,
But allow me one tender kiss-

Placed upon the cheek,
That teardrops dried,
For it will be my final wish;

My lady, My love,
Your song shall never die,
For this ending knows of love:

Nothing shall ever,
Invade the sky,
If it be not from truth above;

My lady, My love,
The world is now your doorstep,
Use it as you will:

 For I am just a servant,
Waiting for your song,
And I offer to you all I have to give;

My lady, My love,
With the ground as my witness,
And the sky as your door-

The song you sing for me this day,
Shall be all I desire,
And nothing more;

My lady, My love,
My sweet encore,
It shall be all I desire,
And nothing more.

Tantalizing

A tower of snow with chocolate crown,
But no whip cream topping be seen,
A ripened cherry neatly placed-
Like a diamond studded broach,
On the gown of a queen;

Pecan sprinkles garnish the top,
A rainbow of clouds surrounds the broach,
Strawberry stains trace the fudge,
And the vanilla cream is beyond reproach;

The succulent cherry is devoured first,
Then a sprinkle or two to tease the tongue,
The strawberry stains pose no threat,
For the deed at hand needs be done;

The fudge itself is smooth and warm,
As its shell is pierced ever so slow,
What hides beneath – a glorious sight,
A gentle hand in a raging storm;

Slowly consuming the outer realm,
Until everything is vacant and gone,
A silky white mist be the only remnant left,
By that exotic sundae that pleased the crown.

Fond Wishes

To place a ring upon your hand,
And have you declare your love as mine,
Would be my only wish or dream,
My final plea of fond desire.

To see a smile so vibrant and sweet,
I would lay my life in your hands,
I would take my place beneath your feet,
And proclaim you queen of nature's land.

Never A Day

One day when the winds blow cold,
One day when the birds do not sing,
That day when wise men grow old;
One morning when the sun prolongs it's time,
One morning when sea bellows ring,
That morning when stars no longer shine:

One afternoon when it rains,
One afternoon when a rainbow dies,
That afternoon when all the seasons change;
One evening when mockingbirds clip their wings,
One evening when turtle doves cry,
That evening when sirens no longer sing:

One night when the ground crumbles 'neath your feet,
One night when the forest no longer sees,
That night that begins eternity;
The hour when all has been conceived,
The hour when the crumbling ground awakes,
There shall you find I bleed:

Then my love, watch the skies,
Let the wind dry your eyes,
For if you search you shall find,
That never a day shall I be not thine.

Another Life

When dismal clouds form overhead,
And the sun struggles to show its' light-
There's only one portrait that hangs on the wall;

When all the world's children have been fed,
And the moon no longer controls the night-
This is when the portrait shall fall;

Leaving its' place without regret,
Leaving a bare scene in reply-
Merely to leap into my hands;

Moving ever so gently without fret,
Placing it upon a pedestal high-
Only to watch it bleed from the stand.

I Thought You Be My Victory

I thought you be my victory
That final soothing-
Of a war-torn soul;
Years and years have I labored,
Bloodied hands from dusk 'til dawn:

I thought you be my victory
That final soothing-
Of a war-torn soul;
Years and years have I labored,
But only to see the curtain drawn;

I thought you be my victory,
I thought you be the one,
I thought you be my victory,
I thought you be my sun;
Years and years have I labored-
Awaiting the day your love stole mine:

I thought you be my victory,
That final soothing-
Of a war-torn soul;
Years and years have I labored,
And now shalt never die in your arms;

I thought you be my victory
That awaited mending-
Of a shattered life;
Instead you be my failure-
Another star for a tortured soul:

I thought you be my victory,
But once again I've thought wrong,

Now here I stand-
A man revered:
A man who labored-
And now dies alone.

A Wish Not Granted

Have I ever told you,
That the time we spend together,
I wish it would last forever and a day?

In your arms I've found,
Everything I've been looking for,
I don't need anything else,
I won't ask for anything more;

In your eyes I see,
My destiny,
To be with you for a lifetime-
Is where I want to be;

As days come in and days go out,
As night settles in,
All I've ever wanted,
Was to be more than just friends;

As my arms embrace you,
And my warm eyes caress you,
Only one thing keeps going through my mind-

Have I ever told you,
That the time we spend together,
I wish it would last forever and a day?

As we continue on,
Leading our own lives,
Wouldn't it be great,
To be side by side;

From one day to the next,
There's nothing that I would regret,
As I reminisce upon the day,
The day when we first met;

I looked into your eyes,
And there I found,
Everything that I would ever need;

When I see you passing by,
With a star in your eye,
I think back upon the time,
When it was just you and I-

And I wonder if I ever told you,
That the time we spent together,
I wished it would last forever and a day?

But I guess it wasn't meant to be,
As I look back on reality-
A smile appears on your face,
And a tear dims my eye;

And I wish I would have told you,
That the times we spent together,
I wanted them to last forever and a day.

Cosmic Embrace

Never before have I seen such a view,
A sea of stars, with silver light.
Eyes made out of starlight, emerald blue,
Gleam through the darkness of the night.

A marbled plate colored tempest hue,
Drawn to the light of a distant day,
An attraction for a wanderer's love anew,
A heart once lost now finds its way.

The world spins slowly, yet never still,
A wanderer's love now found anew.
In the heavens, where dreams come true,
In the embrace of a cosmic will.

The Weight of Sound

In every note, a sorrow flows,
A melody carved from silent grief;
Through threads of sound, the heart bestows,
A music shaped by shadows deep.
The chords emerge like whispered sighs,
Each line a mirror of the soul—
A truth that words could never hold,
A weight that lingers past the notes,
As if despair itself could sing.

Sonnet 8

A morbid statue unsuppressed,
By anything that has no means,
An incandescent pictured crest,
That no more has fulfilling dreams;

As draped in cloth from port to bow,
With strings of beads around the throne,
A kiss is placed upon the brow,
While moonlight shines from where unknown;

The stars have then become the eyes,
As rings emerge from overhead,
There is to be to no surprise,
Another bloom upon the bed:

The youthfulness engaged upon,
Be beams that yield from great beyond.

To make a wish upon a star,
Above illustrious mother earth,
Would be to me a dream-filled scar,
To see a falling man's rebirth.

To have that wish fulfilled that night,
To finally gain a man's reprise,
Would be to me the ultimate high,
To see a star that streaks the skies;

To reach beyond that mortal plane,
Where wise of men have always gone,
To stretch my heart and feel the pain,
That somewhere out there found a home;

To see again a sunset fall,
In which the moon doth tell it all.

Sonnet 21

The muse, the stage, the stagecraft blues,
Leaves nothing left for puppeteers,
From Thespis histrionics flow,
Extravaganza – harlequin;

The trilogy through monologue,
Morality play, opera,
An interlude to separate,
The masque, ballet and theatrics;

From pantomime to epilogue,
From music hall to silver screen,
From stalls and boxes, orchestra,
From Pantaloon to shooting star:

To be or not to be serene,
Leaves no man without dramas dream.

Untitled 42

Scented candles, decorative sense,
Calming winds, raining mists,
Red dipped blades, candles out,
Calm winds stop, frozen teardrops.

Sonnet 7

Hand in hand one breath we breathe,
As ocean waves upon the shore,
It is for this that we reprieve,
To hope and wish, then ask for more;

The ocean then begins to rise,
As one small boat is set adrift,
To raise its flag and cloud the skies,
Another fault begins to shift;

From left to right the waters roll,
Within, without the boat withstands,
The very nature of the scroll,
To place itself upon the land;

The tides rushed in and overcame,
The one small boat that did the same.

115

As I look into your eyes,
I see the ocean's deepest hue,
And as I kiss your tender lips,
I know I shall never love but you.

Afterword

As I close this chapter of *The Presence of Knowing: A Poetic Journey of Life*, I am reminded of the profound beauty in sharing the human experience. This collection began as a reflection of my own path—one filled with love and loss, the quiet wisdom of nature, the echoes of self-discovery, and the ever-present musings of life's finite nature. Yet, in offering these words to the world, I've discovered something even greater: the universal connection that exists in our shared truths.

To each of you who have journeyed through these pages, thank you for allowing these poems to be a part of your life. Poetry has a way of illuminating the corners of our souls, uncovering emotions we may not have known were there. My hope is that *The Presence of Knowing* has touched your heart, reminded you of your strength, and encouraged you to embrace the light within.

As you step forward from these pages, may the words linger like a soft melody—a quiet reminder that healing, understanding, and connection are always within reach. Life's journey is filled with uncertainty, but it is also rich with moments of clarity, love, and resilience.

Above all, may you carry with you the knowledge that we are never truly alone. Whether in the stillness of reflection, the embrace of community, or the whispered truths of our own hearts, there is always a presence guiding us—a knowing that brings us back to ourselves.

With gratitude and hope,

John David Smith